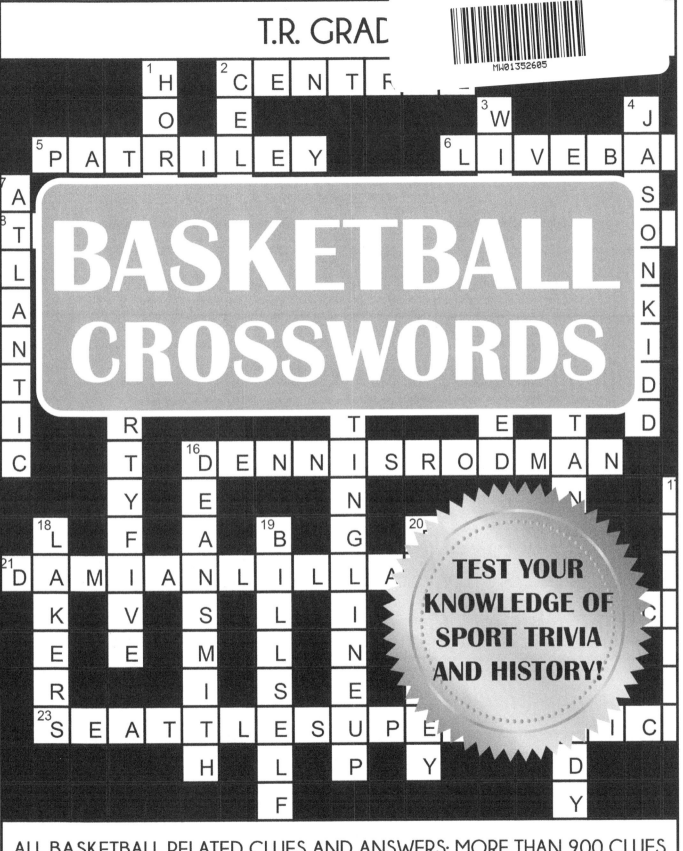

Published by Dylanna Press an imprint of Dylanna Publishing, Inc.
Copyright © 2022 by Dylanna Press

Author: T.R. Grady

All rights reserved. No part of this publication may be reproduced, stored in a retrieval system, or transmitted by any means, including electronic, mechanical, photocopying, or otherwise, without prior written permission of the publisher.

Limit of liability/Disclaimer of Warranty: The Publisher and the author make no representations or warranties with respect to the accuracy or completeness of the contents of this work and specifically disclaim all warranties, including without limitation warranties of fitness for a particular purpose.

Although the publisher has taken all reasonable care in the preparation of this book, we make no warranty about the accuracy or completeness of its content and, to the maximum extent permitted, disclaim all liability arising from its use.

This book is not endorsed by and is not associated with National Basketball Association.

Trademarks: Dylanna Press is a registered trademark of Dylanna Publishing, Inc. and may not be used without written permission.

Puzzle #1

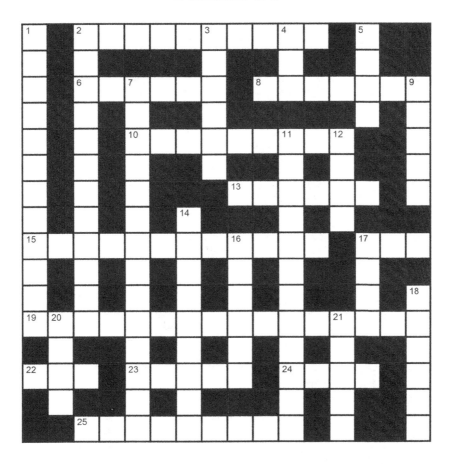

Across

2 Side of the court containing the live ball (6,4)
6 PHI, Joel (6)
8 1st Mavs player to make an all star team, 1984, Mark (7)
10 Bucks record for most steals in a game, Alvin (9)
13 CHI, Zach (6)
15 Inducted into HOF as player and coach, ATL, SEA, 1979 NBA champion (5,7)
17 One on one defense (3)
19 2017 MVP OKC (7,9)
22 Karl-Anthony Towns nickname (3)
23 BOS, Jayson (5)
24 Most points in a single game Bucks history, 2006, Michael (4)
25 Clippers coach (6,3)

Down

1 Pacers player who frequently trash talked Spike Lee at Knicks games (6,6)
2 2000 Co-Roy HOU (5,7)
3 OKC, Josh (6)
4 76ers mascot animal (3)
5 Titles Lakers won in the 1960s (4)
7 Nets arena (8,6)
9 Knicks, HOF, Patrick (5)
11 Most wins regular season history (7,5)
12 Lakers mascot (4)
14 Bucks, Khris (9)
16 Abdul-Jabbar (6)
17 Carmelo Anthony nickname (4)
18 Most assists in a game by a player, 30, Scott (6)
20 Jazz (4)
21 1994 slam dunk champ, MIN, Isaiah (5)

Puzzle #2

Across

4 1965 MVP BOS (4,7)
9 Layup alternative (4,4)
10 1st non white player in NBA, Wataru (6)
12 FSU Coach (7,8)
14 Rebound by defensive player (9,7)
16 Zion (10)
18 A shot deflected by another player (5)
20 2007 ROY POR (7,3)
21 2010 ROY SAC (6,5)
22 WAS, Bradley (4)

Down

1 MIN, GS, Andrew (7)
2 HOF college coach, Louisville, Kentucky, Iona (4,6)
3 IND, Tyrese (10)
5 Beat the Magic in the 2009 Finals (3,7,6)
6 Magic rookie voted an all star starter (4)
7 Tallest player in Hawks history, Priest (9)
8 Scottie Bulls (6)
9 Pacers, Kings Domantas (7)
11 Clippers original team name (6)
13 J.J., Duke, Clippers, ESPN (6)
15 1957 MVP BOS (3,5)
17 CLE, Evan (6)
19 1987 DPOY, LAL, Michael (6)

Puzzle #3

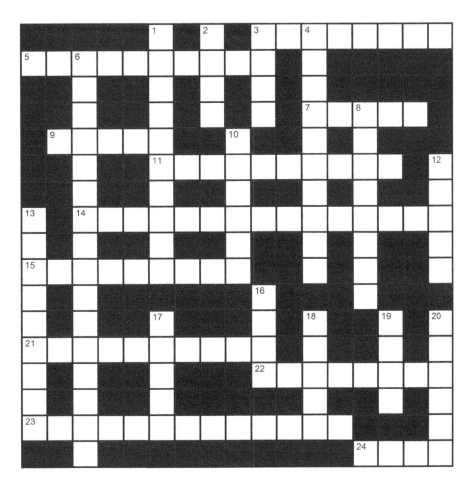

Across

3 OKC, Chet (8)
5 1996 ROY TOR Damon (10)
7 Celtics hold the record for most consecutive championships in US Pro sports history with ____ (5)
9 James Harden facial hair (5)
11 Spurs (3,7)
14 A foul on purpose (11,4)
15 2005 and 2006 MVP Suns (5,4)
21 2008 MVP LAL (4,6)
22 When player jumps up and throws ball down into hoop (4,4)
23 Made playoffs every year from 2004 - 2013 but never reached Finals (6,7)
24 Founded in 1968 Bucks and _____ (4)

Down

1 NBA commisioner from 1984 - 2014 (5,5)
2 Yao (4)
3 MIA (4)
4 2021 ROY Hornets (6,4)
6 Rebound by offensive player (9,7)
8 1981 ROY, UTA, Darrell (8)
10 HOF Celtic, Robert (6)
12 3rd overall pick 2000, Darius (5)
13 1995 CO-ROY DAL (5,4)
16 John Calipari coached this NBA team (4)
17 1st 76ers player to have number retired, Hal (5)
18 Number one ____ pick (5)
19 Suns PG, Chris (4)
20 LAL (6)

Puzzle #4

Across

1. 24 second (4,5)
6. Lost 1976 Finals to BOS (4)
7. Oscar (9)
9. Steph Curry dad (4)
10. MARQ (9)
11. Milwaukee (5)
13. Small sharp step with non- pivot foot towards defending player (3,4)
15. Celtics mascot (10)
17. The floor the game is played on (5)
19. Carrying the ball (7)
20. HOF coach, current announcer, Hubie (5)
21. WVU coach (3,7)
22. Kareem's number (6,5)

Down

1. Won 1986 slam dunk contest, ATL (4,4)
2. LaMelo Ball brother (5)
3. Bucks, Lakers HOF #33 (6,5-6)
4. 1971 CO ROY POR, Geoff (6)
5. Beat the Magic in the 1995 NBA Finals (7,7)
6. Donald Earl Watts nickname, shaved head (5)
8. NYK, RJ (7)
12. Lakers arena sponsor (6)
14. The logo (5,4)
16. Nuggets, Alex (7)
18. Sacramento (5)

Puzzle #5

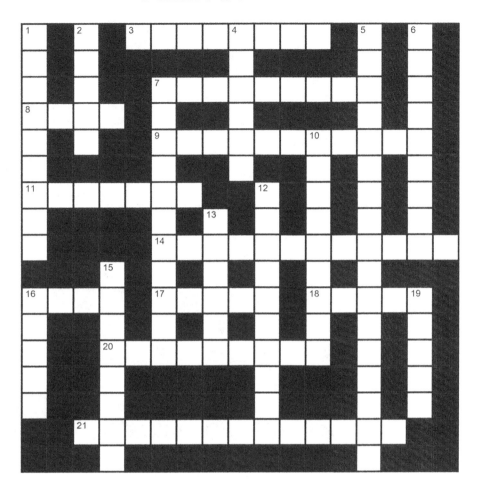

Across

3 2002 ROY Memphis (3,5)
7 Dirk (9)
8 Bill Walton college (4)
9 1984 and 1985 6th man of the year, BOS (5,6)
11 Atlanta Hawks orginal city (7)
14 Kentucky coach (4,8)
16 MEM, Desmond (4)
17 Lakers and Wizards, Kyle (5)
18 1986 ROY, NYK, Patrick (5)
20 76ers coach (3,6)
21 Harlem (13)

Down

1 Only player to retire with more blocked shots than points scored (6,3)
2 Chicago (5)
4 NBA 75 Team, Paul (6)
5 Beat the Lakers in the 1983 NBA Finals (12,5)
6 Highest 3 point FG % Cavs history (5,4)
7 2021 and 2022 MVP DEN (6,5)
10 Cleveland (9)
12 Kings (10)
13 First chinese player to play in NBA, Wang (6)
15 A ball that is not in play (4,4)
16 Badly missed shot (5)
19 HOU, Jalen (5)

Puzzle #6

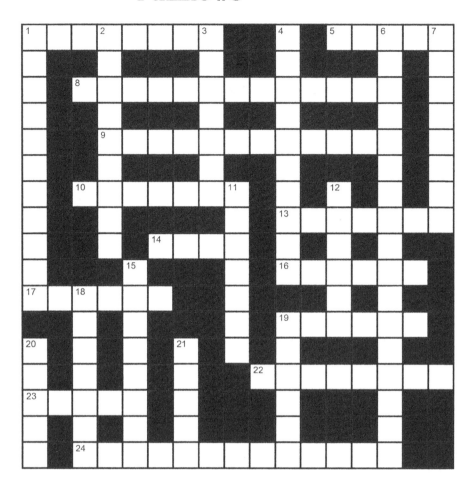

Across

1 TOR, Fred (8)
5 Atlanta (5)
8 Won the 1973 NBA Finals vs LAL (3,4,6)
9 2007 MVP DAL (4,8)
10 1992 ROY Hornets, Larry (7)
13 Rockets (7)
14 1967 ROY, DET, David (4)
16 Bucks single season OREB record, Moses (6)
17 Bulls, Dennis (6)
19 PUR (6)
22 Nets (8)
23 Kemba Walker college (5)
24 Grizzlies coach (6,7)

Down

1 1999 ROY TOR (5,6)
2 Another name for a basket (5,4)
3 Raptors (7)
4 NBA 75 Team, PHI, Billy (10)
6 Beat SEA in the 1978 NBA Finals (10,7)
7 John, Utah (8)
11 Denver (7)
12 Gordon Hayward college (6)
15 Jeff, coach and announcer (3,5)
18 Pistons (7)
19 1987 ROY, IND, Chuck (6)
20 ATL, Trae (5)
21 Bucks mascot (5)

Puzzle #7

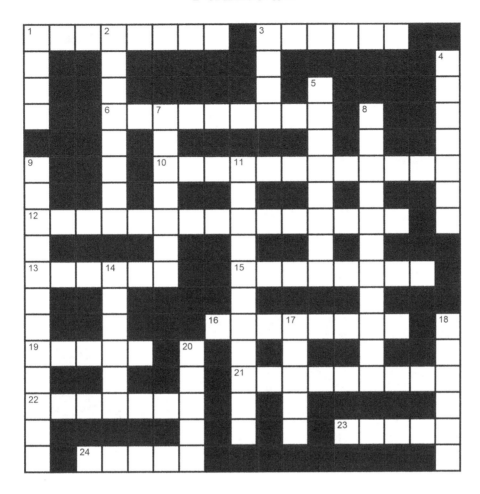

Across

1. Using body to block opponent (8)
3. Mavericks (6)
6. Play by play announcer of NBA Finals (4,5)
10. Sixers #6 HOF, 11x all star, 1x champion (6,6)
12. 1st Heat player to record 1,000 points and 1,000 rebounds in a season (6,9)
13. 1994 Knicks guard, John (6)
15. 1957 ROY, BOS, Tommy (8)
16. Phil Jackson rings (8)
19. 2007 DPOY DEN, Marcus (5)
21. Clippers owner Steve Ballmer used to be CEO of….... (9)
22. Called to stop a game (7)
23. No 2 Pick in 1984, Sam (5)
24. Suns Deandre (5)

Down

1. CHA, LaMelo (4)
2. 1983 ROY, Clippers, Terry (8)
3. Blue Devils (4)
4. Suns, Mikal (7)
5. Magic 1st ever draft pick, Nick (8)
7. Celtics coach with highest career winning percentage .751 (2,5)
8. 1973 MVP BOS (5,6)
9. Most steals NBA history (4,8)
11. DET career leader in points, assists, and steals (5,6)
14. Thunder mascot name (6)
17. Nuggets mascot name (5)
18. CHI, MIN, PHI, MIA Jimmy (6)
20. 1989 DPOY, UTA, Mark (5)

Puzzle #8

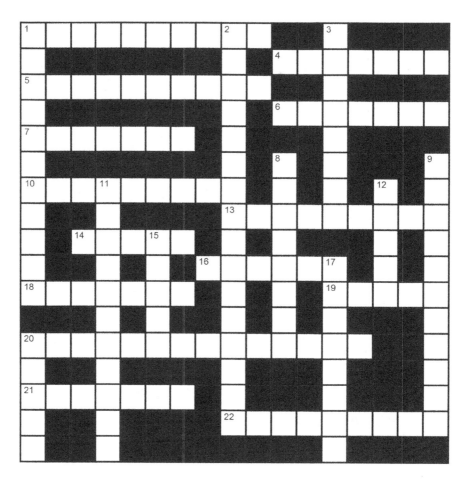

Across

1. Duke _____ (4,6)
4. "Havlicek stole _____" (3,4)
5. A pass that hits the floor (6,4)
6. Dennis Rodman played here before joining the Bulls (7)
7. Tallest player in Rockets history (3,4)
10. Raptors coach (4,5)
13. 1984, 1985, and 1986 MVP (5,4)
14. Shot that bounces off rim or backboard and doesn't go in (5)
16. A pass that leads to a basket (6)
18. An official temporary suspension of the game (7)
19. An advance towards the basket with the ball (5)
20. UNLV, Tark the Shark, 1990 national title (5,9)
21. 2003 No 2 pick, Darko (7)
22. Nets coach (5,4)

Down

1. Indiana coach, 3 national titles, undefeated team 1976 (5,6)
2. Won their 3rd straight title in 2002 (3,7,6)
3. Karl-Anthony Towns college (8)
8. 3rd overall pick 2006, Adam (8)
9. Celtics HOF coach, victory cigar (3,8)
11. 2012 ROY CLE (5,6)
12. Heat (5)
15. Floor on which game is played (5)
17. Celtics arena (2,6)
20. MIA, CLE, LAL, LeBron (5)

Puzzle #9

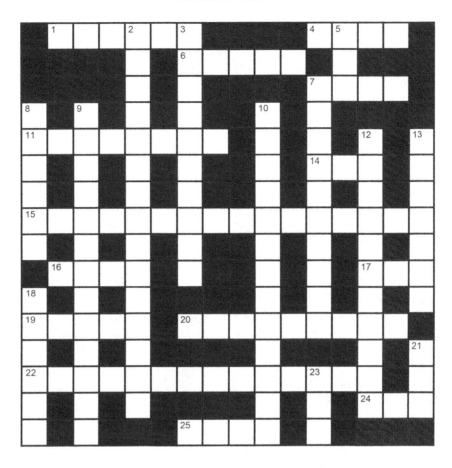

Across

1. Globetrotters (6)
4. Splash brothers, Steph and _____ (4)
6. OKC, Serge (5)
7. Phoenix (4)
11. UCONN women's coach, Geno (8)
14. Scoring titles MJ won (3)
15. Averaged triple double in 2017 season (7,9)
16. HOF Chris, TOR, MIA (4)
17. Hangs from the rim (3)
19. Cavs, Jarrett (5)
20. Basketball movie about college coach starring Nick Nolte (4,5)
22. Beat the Lakers in the 2004 Finals (7,7)
24. Championships Bulls won during the 1990s (3)
25. A player that is unguarded is _____ (4)

Down

2. Blew in LeBrons ear, Pacers (5,10)
3. 2001 ROY Orlando (4,6)
5. Ben Simmons college (3)
7. "Taking my talents to _____" (5,5)
8. Los Angeles (6)
9. Heat coach (4,9)
10. Birdman (5,8)
12. A pass to another player from the sideline (7,4)
13. Jimmy Butler, Jimmy _____ (7)
18. Thunder, Rockets, Nets, Sixers, James (6)
21. Heat arena (3)
23. Allen Iverson drafted number ___ overall (3)

Puzzle #10

Across

1. First black player drafted into the NBA (5,6)
5. IND, LAC, Paul (6)
7. The round mound of rebound, Charles (7)
8. Raptors OG (7)
10. Played with face mask on, nicknamed Rip, DET (7,8)
12. Hawks career scoring leader (9,7)
16. Only player to lead league in blocks and rebounds, ORL (6,6)
19. Red Mamba (4,6)
20. Tallest player in NBA history, Gheorghe (7)
21. MIN, Karl (7,5)
22. Pacers, Magic, Heat, Victor (7)
23. SAC (5)

Down

1. Cedric Maxwell nickname (9)
2. 1999 MVP Utah (4,6)
3. Magic (7)
4. No. 1 pick, Anthony, CLE (7)
6. Only 3x dunk contest champ, Nate (8)
9. Basketball hall of fame (8)
11. 2001 MVP PHI (5,7)
13. 1998 No 1 pick, Michael (10)
14. 1st player to make 200 3 pointers in a season, NYK John (6)
15. Pacers (7)
17. Scored 73 points in a game vs DET in 1978, David (8)
18. NBA 75 Team, Celtics C, Dave (6)

Puzzle #11

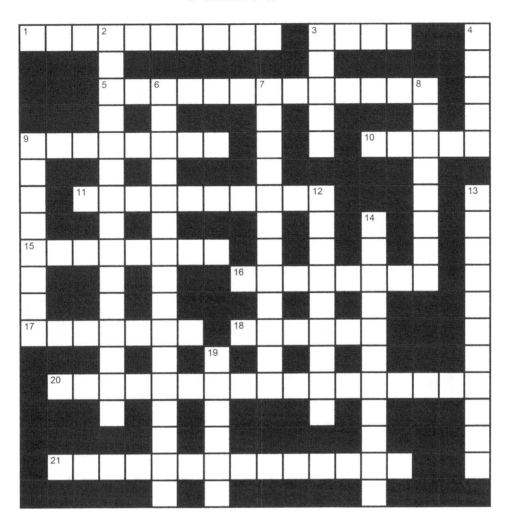

Across

1 A player who comes in to replace another (10)
3 Utah (4)
5 Won the 1970 NBA Finals vs LAL (3,4,6)
9 2012 DPOY, NYK, Tyson (8)
10 PHI, Tyrese (5)
11 To have the ball (10)
15 New Orleans (8)
16 1992 DPOY, SAS, David (8)
17 Rockets "Twin Towers" Olajuwon and _____ (7)
18 TOR, Scottie (6)
20 1980 MVP LAL (6,5-6)
21 Melo (7,7)

Down

2 Won 2014 Finals vs MIA (3,7,5)
3 Pelicans, Herb (5)
4 Bucks 3 point accuracy record, Dell (5)
6 76ers arena (5,5,6)
7 Spurs, Raptors, Clippers, 2x Finals MVP (5,7)
8 First player off the bench (5,3)
9 Los Angeles, not the Lakers (8)
12 76ers original name (9)
13 NBA Finals trophy (5,6)
14 1982 and 1983 MVP PHI and HOU (5,6)
19 HOF Elgin (6)

Puzzle #12

Across

1 Kings original city (6,4)
4 Sharp shooter, Kyle (6)
6 Hondo (4,8)
8 Starred in Uncle Drew (5,6)
9 Famous rapper who is big Raptors fan (5)
11 First Celtic to block more than 200 shots in a season (6,6)
15 1st Cavs player with 200+ 3 pointers in a season, 2016 (2,5)
17 2014 MVP OKC (5,6)
21 Offensive area running from mid-court to end line (5,5)
22 Ball that misses hoop and backboard (7)
23 2017 DPOY GS (8,5)

Down

2 2021 6th man of the year, Utah, Jordan (8)
3 2022 6th man of the year, MIA (5,5)
5 UVA (8)
7 2016 ROY MIN (4-7,5)
9 2009, 2010, and 2011 DPOY ORL (6,6)
10 Player passes ball to teammate that leads to basket (6)
12 Minnesota (12)
13 NBA 75 Team, Elvin, WASH (5)
14 Walt Frazier nickname (5)
16 Coach stands here (8)
18 SAS, ATL, Dejounte (6)
19 Positioning between basket and opponent to obtain rebound (3,3)
20 WNBA, Brittney (6)

Puzzle #13

Across

1. Jump that starts the game (3,3)
4. "Sid the Squid" Bucks, Sidney (8)
6. Orlando (5)
9. Pelicans, Lakers, Forward, 2020 champion (7,5)
12. MIA career points leader (6,4)
14. 76ers (12)
15. Longest winning streak ever, 1971-1972 LAL (6,5)
17. DPOY Gary (6)
18. Mid-court mark (4,4)
19. New York (6)
20. HOF Tracy (7)

Down

2. 2nd overall pick in 1991, CLE, Danny (5)
3. KU (6)
4. MSU (8,5)
5. Lakers old arena name (7,6)
6. The Lakers won 5 of their titles when they played in this city (11)
7. Most blocks in single season in Nets history, 1978 (6,7)
8. Won 2008 Finals vs LAL (6,7)
10. 2012 6th man of the year, OKC (5,6)
11. Youngest player to lead league in rebounding (6,6)
13. DET, Cade (10)
16. ATL (5)

Puzzle #14

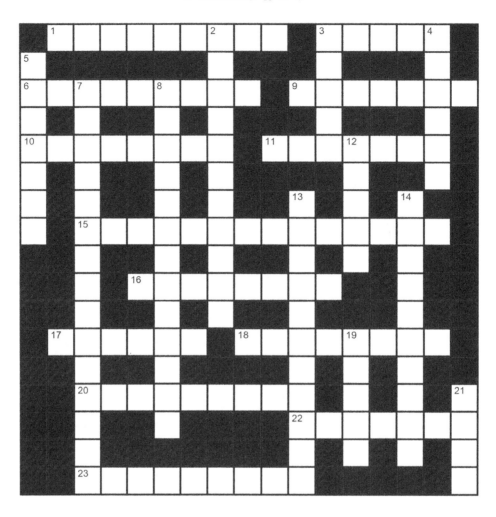

Across

1. Won 1st ever MVP award in 1956 (3,6)
3. ORL (5)
6. Kyrie Irving movie (5,4)
9. CLE, Darius (7)
10. A foul ruled to be excessive (8)
11. Bouncing the ball on the court (7)
15. 1993 MVP Suns (7,7)
16. 76ers record for most 3 pointers in a season, 2019 (2,6)
17. Pelicans mascot name (6)
18. Jordan retired to play (8)
20. 2011 6th man of the year, LAL (5,4)
22. Hawks (7)
23. Hawks division (9)

Down

2. During the 2012-2013 season the Heat won _____ games in a row (6,5)
3. Michael Jordan has his number retired in Chicago and _____ (5)
4. Longtime Grizzlies PG, Mike (6)
5. Clippers original city (7)
7. Mr. Big Shot (8,7)
8. Most rebounds Clippers history (7,6)
12. Kareem original team (5)
13. 2022 DPOY (6,5)
14. Pelicans (3,7)
19. CHI (5)
21. UTA (4)

Puzzle #15

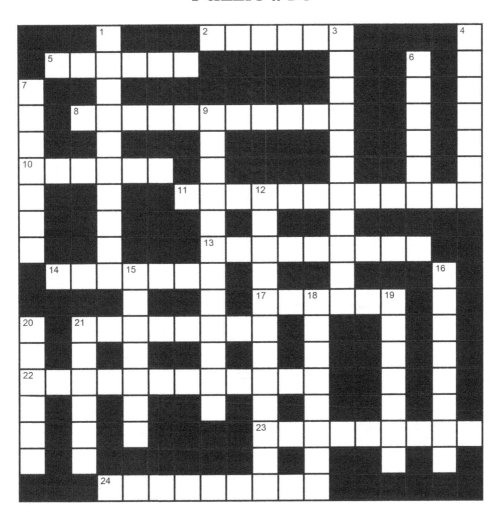

Across

2 Had 2 quadruple doubles in one month, HOU (6)
5 2x 6th man of the year, Ricky (6)
8 NBA 75 Team, NY, Dave (11)
10 1955 ROY, Hawks, Bob (6)
11 Two-handed overhead shot (8,4)
13 Area of court farthest from offensive team's goal (4,5)
14 UF (7)
17 1971 CO ROY, David (6)
21 Most career 3 point attempts without a make, 0-26, Zaza (8)
22 Clyde the Glide (5,7)
23 A device that keeps track of time left to take a shot (4,5)
24 Came back from 3-1 to win the 2016 Finals (9)

Down

1 Bulls won _____ games in 1995-1996 season (7,3)
3 1979 MVP HOU (5,6)
4 DeMarcus (7)
6 Lakers coach with most championships, John (6)
7 1984 ROY, HOU, Ralph (7)
9 Clippers owner, Microsoft (5,7)
12 Pacers coach, formerly Mavs (4,8)
15 HOU (7)
16 Pistol Pete (8)
18 Golden State (8)
19 MIA player nicknamed "The Spin Doctor" Ron (7)
20 Indiana (6)
21 SEA Gary (6)

Puzzle #16

Across

1 1995 DPOY DEN, Dikembe (7)
3 Grizzlies division (9)
6 Hawks career leader in blocks, Tree (7)
9 2011 MVP CHI (7,4)
10 The team who doesn't have the ball is on (7)
11 1st teenager to score 20+ points in 10 straight games, NO (4,10)
13 2022 ROY TOR (7,6)
15 2009 no 2 pick, Hasheem (7)
16 Coached the Miami Heat to a championship in 2006 (3,5)
18 Antetokounmpo (7)
19 1995 MVP SAN (5,8)
20 Ray Allen original team (5)
21 BOS Jaylen (5)
22 Bulls coach (5,7)

Down

1 Mavs owner, shark tank (4,5)
2 Magic, Paolo (8)
3 Amar'e (10)
4 1966, 1967, and 1968 MVP PHI (4,11)
5 Won the NBA Finals in 1967 vs LAL (7-6)
7 NYK player most points in single game (7,7)
8 1st Hornet to block more than 250 shots in a season, 1993, Alonzo (8)
12 "Nate the Great" number retired by GS and CLE (4,8)
14 Oklahoma City (7)
17 NYK (6)
18 2017 6th man of the year, HOU Eric (6)

Puzzle #17

Across

1. 2001 No 1 Pick, Kwame (5)
3. Area close to the basket (3,4)
7. Also called palming (8)
9. 2011 ROY LAC (5,7)
11. 1978 MVP POR (4,6)
13. 2013 no 1 pick, Anthony (7)
14. Most three pointers in NBA debut (7), 2019, Hornets (2,10)
16. Sixers and Nets, Ben (7)
19. 2008 ROY SEA (5,6)
20. Single season record for offensive rebounds, Rockets (5,6)
21. Nickname "Black Jesus" Earl (6)
22. Dwyane Wade played on the Heat and the _____ (5)
23. Hawks conference (7)
24. IND (6)

Down

1. Celtics (6)
2. Rockets "Twin Towers" Sampson and _____ (8)
4. Nike founder (4,6)
5. 1999 and 2000 DPOY, MIA, Alonzo (8)
6. NOP (8)
7. Lakers share an arena with the….. (8)
8. Timelord (6,8)
10. Warriors (6,5)
12. When offensive team gives ball to defensive team (8)
15. Only franchise to not have 60 or more losses in a season (4)
17. MIN coach in 2004 season, won 58 games that year, Flip (8)
18. Team not in possession of ball (7)

Puzzle #18

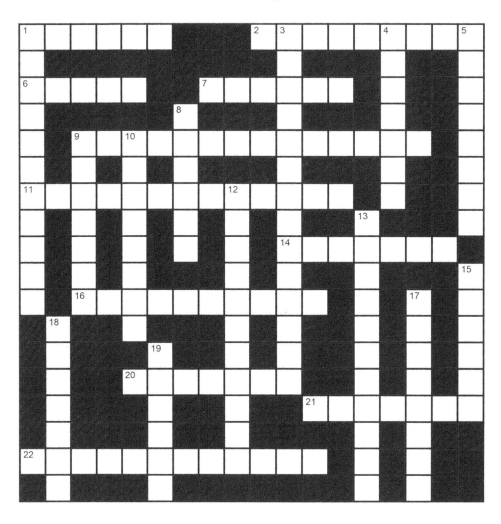

Across

1. Team DET beat to win 1st championship (6)
2. 2006 ROY NO (5,4)
6. Won 2021 Finals vs the Suns (5)
7. 1975 ROY, GS, Jamaal (6)
9. 1993 ROY ORL (9,5)
11. 3x 6th man of the year, not Lou Williams (5,8)
14. Shot that doesn't touch basket or backboard (7)
16. Hakeem Olajuwon # (6,4)
20. TOR, SAS, CHI DeMar (7)
21. Gaining possession of ball after it bounced off backboard on missed shot (7)
22. 1997 ROY PHI (5,7)

Down

1. 2012 and 2013 MVP MIA (6,5)
3. 1994 MVP HOU (6,8)
4. Draymond Green recorded this after every Finals game in 2022 (7)
5. Basketball movie starring Bow Wow (4,4)
8. DEN, Jamal (6)
9. Tennessee women's coach, Pat (7)
10. Celtics division (8)
12. NYK nicknamed Clyde (4,7)
13. Kareem (5,0-0,6)
15. Dwight, Magic (6)
17. Stan, coach and announcer (3,5)
18. Bucks season assist record, Sam (7)
19. NBA 75 Team, Spurs, George (6)

Puzzle #19

Across

3 UTA, MIN Rudy (6)
5 Most fouls in Bulls history (7,6)
9 OKC (7)
10 2019 ROY DAL (4,6)
14 MSG (7,6,6)
16 NOP, LAL, Anthony (5)
18 Basketball movie about Celtics fans (6,5)
20 When player dribbles with two hands or stops and then begins again (6,7)
22 4x DPOY Ben (7)
23 Heat player with highest career FG% (9,5)
24 HOF Warriors, Rick (5)
25 Celtics conference (7)

Down

1 Trail Blazers (8)
2 HOF UCONN coach (3,7)
4 Heat mascot name (6)
6 Bulls (7)
7 Recorded triple dopuble in Finals clinching game, GS (8,5)
8 Suns 6th man of the year, Eddie (7)
11 Portland coach (8,7)
12 Hornets (9)
13 1968 ROY, Bullets, Earl (6)
15 Scored 70 points against the Celtics in 2017 (5,6)
17 Grizzlies original city (9)
19 Chris Paul nickname (5,3)
21 Clyde HOF (7)

Puzzle #20

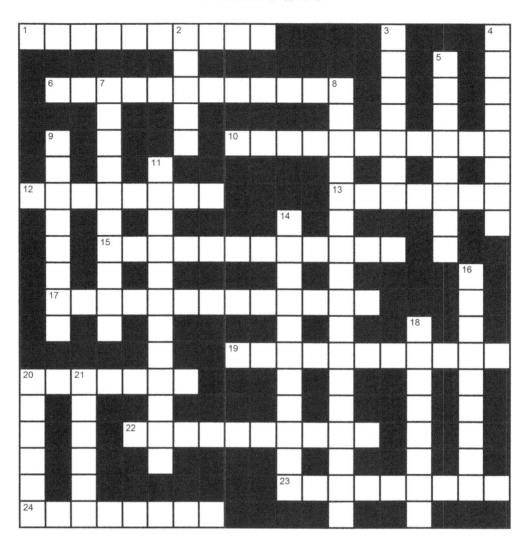

Across

1 Jazz traded this all star C in 2022 (4,6)
6 NYK single season scoring record (7,5)
10 Kareem original name (3,8)
12 Making room for ball handler (5,3)
13 Nets conference (7)
15 Bulls mascot (5,3,4)
17 1998 MVP CHI (7,6)
19 Oldest player to score 20+ points in a game (5,6)
20 Warriors division (7)
22 2018 ROY PHI (3,7)
23 Suns highest single season FT % (5,4)
24 Carmelo Anthony college (8)

Down

2 Swept the Bullets in the 1971 Finals (5)
3 Dominique (7)
4 2020 ROY Memphis (2,6)
5 Shortest dunk contest champion at 5'7 (4,4)
7 Ben Affleck basketball movie (3,3,4)
8 OKC, Shai (8,9)
9 3x 6th man of the year, Lou (8)
11 Celtics all time points leader (4,8)
14 2009 and 2010 MVP CLE (6,5)
16 Also known as endlines (9)
18 Steph, Klay and _____ (8)
20 Malice at the Palace, Pistons vs _____ (6)
21 C (6)

Puzzle #21

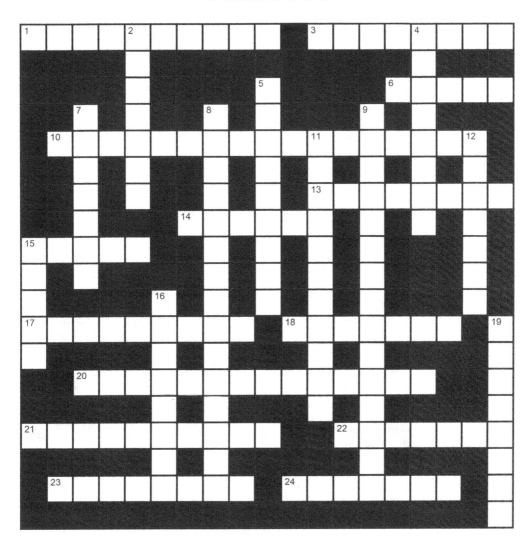

Across

1. UCLA coach, 10 national titles (4,6)
3. Celtics coach (3,5)
6. 1978 ROY, Suns, Walt (5)
10. 1976 and 1977 MVP LAL (6,5-6)
13. 5 seasons with 200+ steals, ATL, Mookie (8)
14. XAV (6)
15. 1966 ROY, Warriors, Rick (5)
17. 1st MIN player with 2,000 points in a season (5,4)
18. Clippers division (7)
20. Duke HOF coach (4,10)
21. Youngest player to record 3 triple doubles (4,6)
22. DEN (7)
23. Area near free throw line (4,4)
24. Made record 10 threes in a half in 2014, HOU, Chandler (7)

Down

2. HOF Lenny (7)
4. Ball that is not in play (4,4)
5. Boundary lines that run length of both sides of court (9)
7. Hornets conference (7)
8. Beat the Heat in the 2011 NBA Finals (6,9)
9. Swept the Cavs in the 2007 Finals (3,7,5)
11. 2004 ROY CLE (6,5)
12. Team that attempted 70 threes in a game in 2019 (7)
15. MIL (5)
16. Play where a pass is thrown to a player in the air who then dunks it (5,3)
19. Shot taken while jumping in the air (4,4)

Puzzle #22

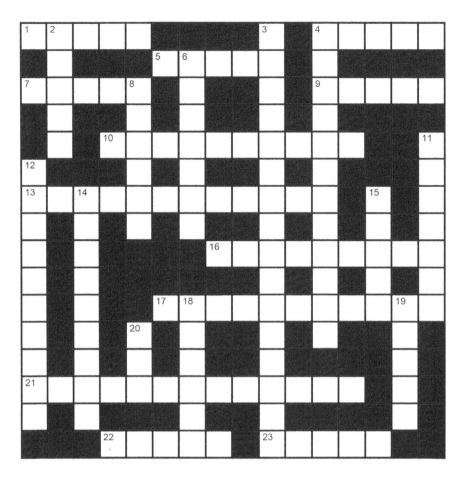

Across

1. San Antonio (5)
4. 1973 ROY, BUF, Sidney (5)
5. 2022 pick 3, HOU, Jabari (5)
7. DEN, Nikola (5)
9. LeBron tosses ____ pregame (5)
10. The Jet, Mavs 6th man (5,5)
13. Knicks coach (3,9)
16. Wood or fiberglass attached to back of basket (9)
17. Pistons coach (6,5)
21. SG (8,5)
22. BOS, Marcus (5)
23. Colored area near the hoop (5)

Down

2. GS, Jordan (5)
3. Wesley Snipes and Woody Harrelson basketball movie (5,3,4,4)
4. Celtics owner (3,9)
6. Dikembe (7)
8. Mike Krzyzewski nickname (5,1)
11. Bucks Jrue, (7)
12. Pistons single season scoring record, Jerry (10)
14. 2013 DPOY MEM (4,5)
15. 1976 ROY, Alvan, Suns (5)
18. Magic, Franz (6)
19. NYK Patrick (5)
20. TV Network Charles Barkley (3)

Puzzle #23

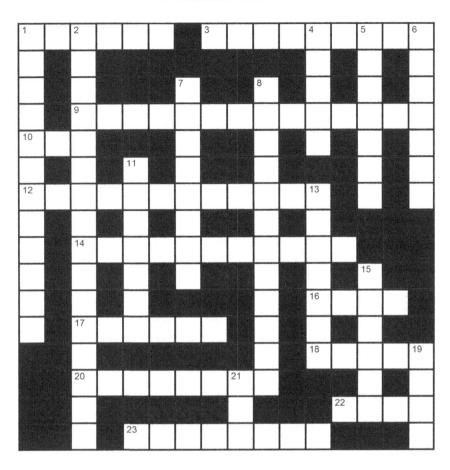

Across

1. Offensive player stands between opponent and teammate to create separation (6)
3. Timberwolves (9)
9. 2000 MVP LAL (9,5)
10. Kamikaze Kid, Ron (3)
12. Thunder (8,4)
14. 2005 ROY Bobcats (5,6)
16. Pistons 2022 pick 5, Jaden (4)
17. Blocking a player to get in rebounding position (3,3)
18. Grizzlies mascot name (5)
20. Extra time in a tied game (8)
22. 2007 No 1 Pick, Greg (4)
23. Looney Tunes Michael Jordan (5,3)

Down

1. SF (5,7)
2. Former OKC PG (7,9)
4. 1985 DPOY, UTA, Mark (5)
5. The team in possesion of the ball is on (7)
6. Rockets coach during 22 game winning streak in 2008, Rick (7)
7. Drafted pick before Giannis, Shabazz (8)
8. FSU (7,5)
11. Suns (7)
13. Tallest player inducted into the HOF (3,4)
15. A segment of the game (6)
19. Defense that isn't one on one (4)
21. 1988 coach of the year, DEN Doug (3)

Puzzle #24

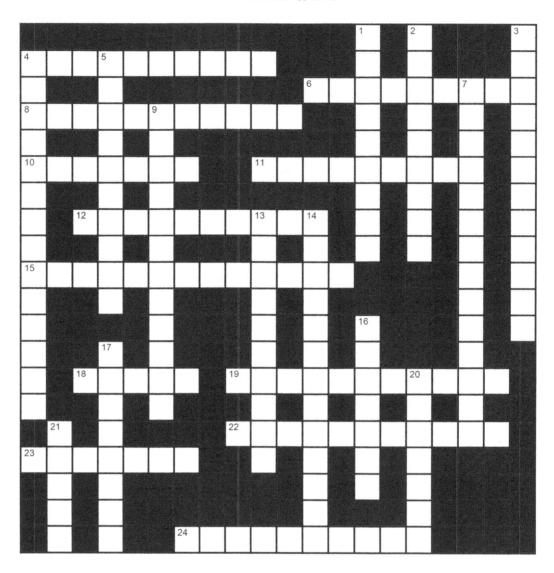

Across

4 Documentary about 2 high school basketball players in Chicago (4,6)
6 1975 MVP Buffalo (3,6)
8 1st OKC player to average 30 points a game (5,6)
10 Cavs conference (7)
11 6th man of the year and most improved player, 1999, Darrell (9)
12 Kangaroo Kid, Billy (10)
15 2015 ROY MIN (6,7)
18 Founded in 1968 Suns and _____ (5)
19 1994 ROY GS, college at Michigan (5,6)
22 A player that gets too many fouls quickly into a game is in…. (4,7)
23 Late 80s early 90s Pistons nickname (3,4)
24 1st Bulls player to have jersey retired, #4 (5,5)

Down

1 1st Hawks player to win MVP (3,6)
2 MEM, Jaren (7,2)
3 In 2022 Kevin Durant requested a trade from this team (8,4)
4 Only player with more than 200 blocks and 200 steals in same season (6,8)
5 Derrick Rose position (5,5)
7 Nets player with most 3 pointers in a season, 2019 (7,7)
9 1st Mavs player to win MVP (4,8)
13 KG drafted out of (4,6)
14 Suns coach (5,8)
16 MIN, Anthony (7)
17 Ball tossed in the air by referee between two players (4,4)
20 DAL, NYK, Jalen (7)
21 Lost 1995 Finals to Rockets (5)

Puzzle #25

Across

1. 1st Hornet to win ROY, 1992 (5,7)
4. Carmelo original team (7)
7. Hornets first ever draft pick, 1988, Rex (7)
9. UNC coach, recently retired (3,8)
11. Beat Spurs in 2013 Finals (5,4)
13. Nuggets division (9)
15. Pistons conference (7)
20. Pistons coach with highest win %, fired after 2008 season (4,8)
21. The Human Highlight Film (7)
22. Most consecutive free throws made in a playoff game (24) 2011 (4,8)
23. 1996 MVP CHI (7,6)
24. "Skywalker" Nuggets (5,8)

Down

2. 1st player in history to have 2,000 pts, 900 assists, and 600 rebounds in a season, HOU (5,6)
3. When the defense guards the team for the entirety of the court (4,5,5)
5. Memphis (9)
6. Michigan State coach (3,4)
8. 1998 ROY SAN (3,6)
10. 2015 and 2016 DPOY SAS (5,7)
12. Blocked 8 shots in a quarter WAS (6,3)
14. HOF player, coach, and announcer, BOS (5,8)
16. Cavs division (7)
17. Pistons coach 1983-1992 (5,4)
18. Oldest player to score 50 points in a game, Jamal (8)
19. DET (7)

Puzzle #26

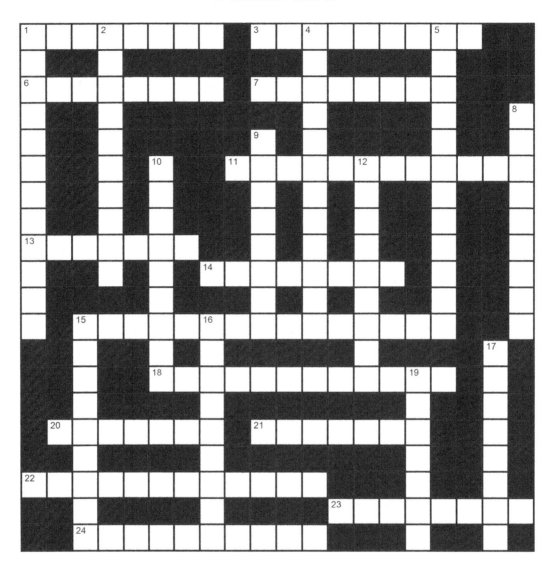

Across

1. Two opposing players attempt to gain possesion of the ball but fail (4,4)
3. 5x champion, 15x all star, 15x all defense, 3x Finals MVP, Forward (3,6)
6. Hit game tying 3 in Game 6 of 2013 Finals vs the Spurs (3,5)
7. Bounces off backboard and in (4,4)
11. 1989 and 1990 MVP LAL (5,7)
13. Using hands to hinder opponent's movement (7)
14. 1st Nets player to win ROY, 1981, Buck (8)
15. 2004 Finals MVP (8,7)
18. Shot from behind the arc (5,7)
20. Boston (7)
21. Charlotte (7)
22. Tallest Mavs player ever, 7 foot 6 (5,7)
23. Beat CLE in 2018 Finals (8)
24. He owns the Cavs (3,7)

Down

1. Hawks macsot (5,3,4)
2. MIA career points leader (6,4)
4. 2008 6th man of the year, SAS (4,8)
5. 1st Pelican with 200 blocks in a season (7,5)
8. Metta World Peace (3,6)
9. Lakers, Knicks, Heat coach, HOF, Heat team president (3,5)
10. Moving from back court toward offensive basket (4,5)
12. Linsanity (6,3)
15. Cavaliers (9)
16. Clippers franchise assist leader (5,4)
17. Most career points among players who never made all star game, Jamal (8)
19. Pacers conference (7)

Puzzle #27

Across

2 Pistons division (7)
5 Future HOF coach who drafted by the Rockets in the 1967 draft (3,5)
6 Ball in play (4,4)
8 Penalty when player moves without dribbling ball (9)
9 Play where player throws ball high and teammate jumps, catches ball, and slams into hoop (5-3)
12 Spurs division (9)
14 Beat the Knicks in the 1994 NBA Finals (7,7)
16 1990 and 1991 DPOY, DET (6,6)
21 2013 ROY POR (6,7)
22 Two teams still in original city, Celtics and _____ (6)
23 Beat WASH in the 1979 NBA Finals (7,11)

Down

1 CHA (7)
2 Won the NBA Finals in 1968 and 1969 (7)
3 1st Knicks MVP (6,4)
4 Mavs coach (5,4)
7 Nets division (8)
10 Lakers division (7)
11 Five players that start a game (8,6)
13 Jordan returned wearing number (5,4)
15 Magic coach from 2007 -2012 (4,3,5)
16 Kansas coach, 11 Final 4s, 2 national titles (4,5)
17 Shortest player in Nets history, 5'5, Earl (7)
18 Knicks beat them to win 1st title (6)
19 Kansas coach (4,4)
20 76ers single season block record, Shawn (7)

Puzzle #28

Across

1. 1993 and 1994 DPOY, HOU (6,8)
4. PG Nets. 10x all star, 1x champion Mavs (5,4)
6. 10x champion, Celtics guard, NBA 75 Team (3,5)
8. MIN (12)
9. When ball bounces off backboard into basket (4,4)
10. MEM (9)
15. 1st Cavs player to win ROY (6,5)
16. Portland (5,7)
17. Heat conference (7)
18. Knicks division (8)
20. Beat GS in the 2019 Finals (7)
21. Played for the Pacers and the Spurs in the same game, 1973, Bob (9)
22. Pacers division (7)
23. A.I. (5,7)
24. Won the 2005 Finals vs DET (3,7,5)

Down

2. When two opposing players jump for ball tossed in air by ref (4,4)
3. Illegally stopping a shot that is on its way down (4,7)
5. 1971 and 1972 MVP Bucks (6,5-6)
7. KG (5,7)
10. Larry Johnson nickname (9)
11. PHI (7-6)
12. Jazz coach (4,5)
13. Violation for taking too long to inbound the ball (4,6)
14. Hornets franchise record for most 3 pointers (5,6)
19. BOS (7)

Puzzle #29

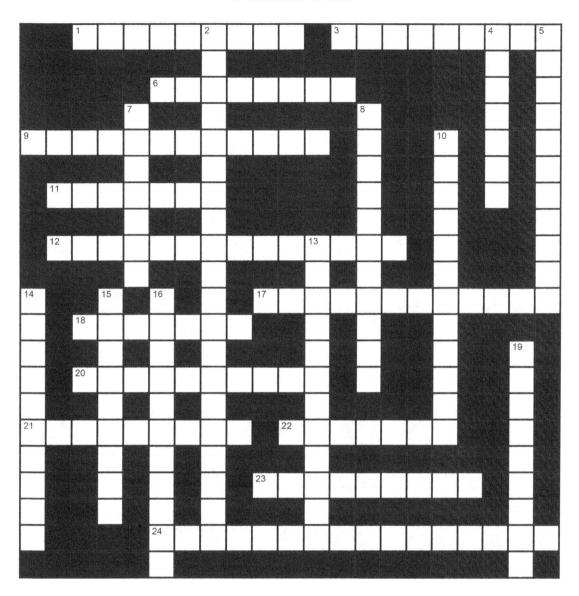

Across

1. 1st ROY in New Orleans history (5,4)
3. Dallas (9)
6. Beat CLE in 2017 Finals (8)
9. Won the first ever NBA Finals in 1947, city (12)
11. Mavericks conference (7)
12. Beat the Lakers in the 1989 NBA Finals (7,7)
17. Won the 1998 NBA Finals vs Utah (7,5)
18. Suns division (7)
20. Prince of Midair (5,1,4)
21. Bought the Dallas Mavericks in 2000 (4,5)
22. Pelicans original name (7)
23. 1986 DPOY, SAS, Alvin (9)
24. Beat the 76ers in the 2001 NBA Finals (3,7,6)

Down

2. Beat PHI in the 1977 NBA Finals (8,5,7)
4. Team Hawks beat to win first championship (7)
5. Ray Allen was traded to the Celtics by the _____ (11)
7. TOR (7)
8. 1st player to lead all players in the Finals in points, rebounds, assists, steals, and blocks (6,5)
10. Shortest player in NBA history at 5'3 (6,6)
13. A player reaches double digits in 3 offensive categories in a game (6,6)
14. 2014 DPOY CHI (6,4)
15. Nets career leader in steals, 2nd all time NBA history (5,4)
16. 1961, 1962, and 1963 MVP (4,7)
19. CLE (9)

Puzzle #30

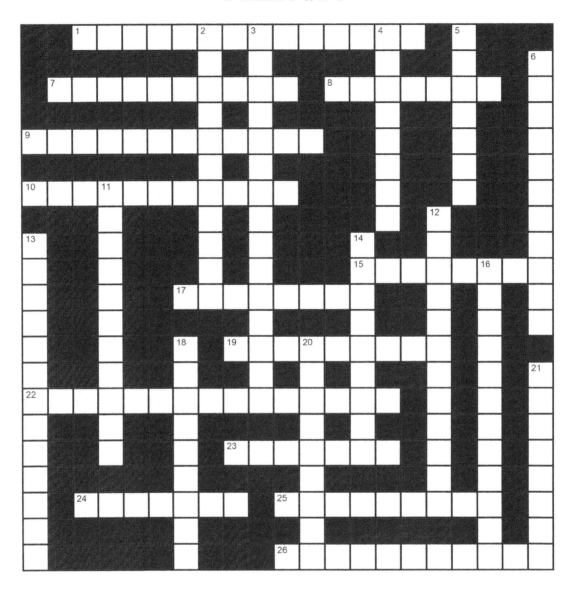

Across

1. Oldest player to record more than 20 rebounds in a game (7,7)
7. Cavs coach with highest win %, 2014-2016 (5,5)
8. Team that drafted 1st black player (7)
9. PF (5,7)
10. Shot deflected on way to basket (7,4)
15. 76ers division (8)
17. LAC (8)
19. Lakers coach (6,3)
22. 1960 MVP PHI (4,11)
23. Washington (7)
24. Bucks conference (7)
25. Pistons original city (4,5)
26. 1988 ROY NY, now an announcer (4,7)

Down

2. 1958 MVP BOS (4,7)
3. Ron Artest (5,5,5)
4. To fake a pass or shot (4,4)
5. Kings division (7)
6. Quickly changing direction (8,3)
11. Warriors arena (5,6)
12. Scored 13 points in the final 35 seconds of a game to beat the Spurs in 2004 (5,7)
13. 1st MIN player to win ROY (6,7)
14. Most 3 pointers in Nets history (5,4)
16. Lost 1990 and 1992 NBA Finals, led by Clyde Drexler (5,7)
18. Won 2012 NBA Finals vs OKC (5,4)
20. NOVA (9)
21. Jesus Shuttlesworth (3,5)

Puzzle #31

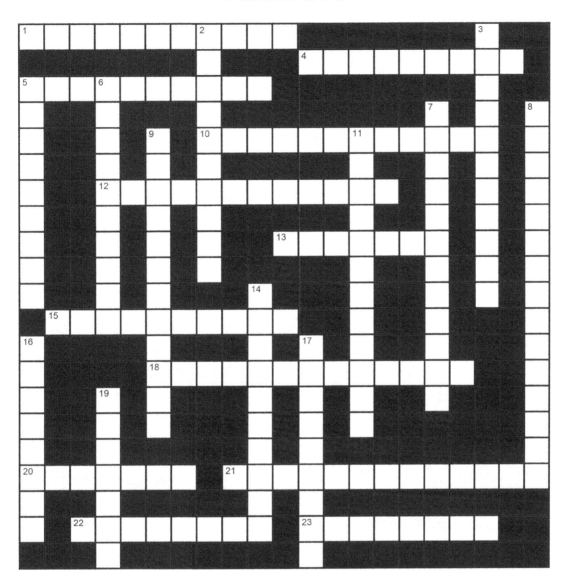

Across

1. Former Warriors coach, now announcer (4,7)
4. Celtics 33 (5,4)
5. Most ever 3 pointers (5,5)
10. Most assists Hornets history (6,6)
12. POR (5,7)
13. WAS (7)
15. 2021 DPOY UTA (4,6)
18. Record for most missed free throws in a game, 23, DET 2016 (5,8)
20. Knicks conference (7)
21. 1986 NBA Finals champs, beat HOU (6,7)
22. Beat CLE in 2015 Finals (8)
23. Raptors division (8)

Down

2. 1997 MVP Utah (4,6)
3. Celtics coach before Ime Udoka (4,7)
5. Mavericks division (9)
6. PG (5,5)
7. Made the dunk mainstream (6,6)
8. Beat the Nets in the 2003 Finals (3,7,5)
9. Magic record for most points in a game, 62 (5,7)
11. oldest player ever drafted (27) CLE 2012 (7,5)
14. Shot attempts after a foul (4,6)
16. Rockets original city (3,5)
17. 1992 US Olympic (5,4)
19. Bucks division (7)

Puzzle #32

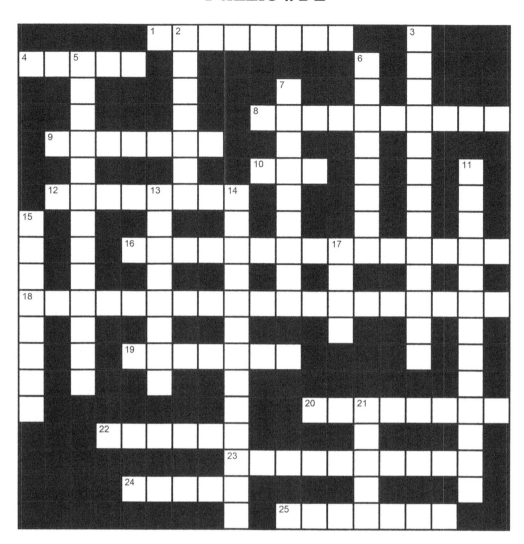

Across

1. Green (8)
4. How many feet wide is a basketball court (5)
8. Robert Horry's nickname (3,4,3)
9. Nuggets conference (7)
10. Julius Erving nickname (2,1)
12. Hakeem Olajuwon nickname (3,5)
16. Scored 100 points in a single game (4,11)
18. Beat the Bullets in the 1975 NBA Finals (6,5,8)
19. First player to score 2000 points in a season, George _____ (7)
20. 2022 Most Improved player (2,6)
22. Generally the tallest player will play _____ (6)
23. 1974 ROY, BUF, Ernie (10)
24. AP player of year, 2020-21, Luke _____ (5)
25. Joel Embiid nickname, The _____ (7)

Down

2. Person who tosses ball up at beginning of game (7)
3. Beat LAL in the 1984 NBA Finals (6,7)
5. The line 15 feet in front of the backboard (4,5,4)
6. AP player of year, 2021-22, Oscar _____ (8)
7. Vinnie Johnson, The _____ (9)
11. 1990 ROY SAN (5,8)
13. Shawn Kemp's nickname (5,3)
14. 1991 and 1992 MVP CHI (7,6)
15. Gary Payton nickname (3,5)
17. Kobe Bryant's middle name (4)
21. Earvin Johnson nickname (5)

Puzzle #33

Across

1. Number of NBA franchises as of 2022 (6)
5. City where NBA was founded (3,4)
10. Larry Bird nickname (5,6)
12. Vince Carter nickname (9)
13. 2015 and 2016 MVP GS (7,5)
15. 2019 and 2020 MVP Bucks (7,13)
16. Bill Walton's school (4)
19. Dennis Rodman's nickname, The _____ (4)
20. Magic conference (7)
22. The Truth (4,6)
23. Home country of Boris Diaw (6)
24. Beat the Jazz in the 1997 NBA Finals (7,5)
25. Nickname of Ben Wallace (3,3)

Down

2. Larry Bird's school (7,5)
3. 2022 Sixth Man of the year (5,5)
4. 2022 Rookie of the year (7,6)
6. MVP of first All-Star Game (2,8)
7. Number of championships won by Celtics, 1957 to 1969 (6)
8. Karl Malone nickname (3,7)
9. OKC single season points record (5,6)
11. Celtic who once led team in all 5 major statistical categories in 1978 (4,6)
14. Warriors original city (12)
17. Robert Parish's nickname (5)
18. AP player of year, 2019-20, Obi _____ (6)
21. George Gervin nickname, The _____ (6)

Puzzle #34

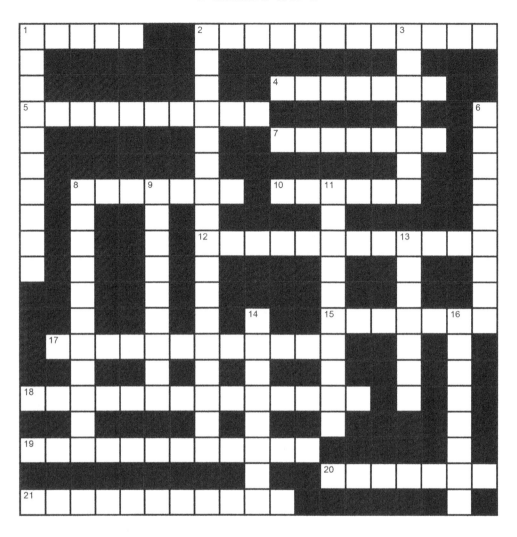

Across

1. Julius Erving drafted by this team but didn't play for them (5)
2. Most 3 pointers in a game (14) (4,8)
4. Area close to the basket (3,4)
5. 1970 MVP NY (6,4)
7. Won MVP, ROY, and all star game MVP in his rookie season, 1970, Spencer (7)
8. Bulls division (7)
10. Rockets beat this team in the 1994 Finals to win their 1st title (6)
12. Bulls single season rebound record (6,6)
15. Bulls conference (7)
17. Al Horford original team (7,5)
18. 1964 MVP Cincinnati (5,9)
19. 1st player to record a quadruple-double (4,8)
20. HOF Walt (7)
21. 1983 NBA scoring title, DEN (4,7)

Down

1. 4x DPOY DET (3,7)
2. 1974 MVP Bucks (6,5-6)
3. Detroit (7)
6. 2002 and 2003 MVP Spurs (3,6)
8. UCONN (11)
9. Media mogul that bought the Hawks in 1977, married Jane Fonda (3,6)
11. Shot from beside or in front of basket (6,4)
13. 1977 ROY, Buffalo, Adrian (7)
14. Won 2022 NBA Finals vs BOS (8)
16. Known for his 3 point shooting, BOS,MIA,SEA, MIL (3,5)

Puzzle #35

Across

3 Sam Perkins nickname (3,6)
8 DAL (9)
9 Knicks arena (7,6,6)
10 1995 CO-ROY DET (5,4)
11 Nickname of Nik Stauskas (5,8)
13 GSW (8)
14 Warriors conference (7)
15 Considered best NBA free-throw shooter (4,5)
16 Number of minutes in college half (6)
19 A ball that is in play (4,4)
20 Pete Maravich's nickname (6,4)
22 Bucks (9)
23 Beat the Mavs in the 2006 Finals (5,4)
24 11 Rings, Celtics (4,7)

Down

1 The Dunkin' Dutchman (3,6)
2 2014 ROY PHI (7,6-8)
4 Illegaly blocking a player (6,6)
5 First non-white player in NBA history (6,6)
6 Line that players shoot from after being fouled (4-5,4)
7 Also called "the one" (5,5)
12 Glen Robinson's nickname (3,3)
17 Allen Iverson nickname (3,6)
18 Two teams still in original city, Knicks and _____ (7)
21 Kenny Smith's nickname (3,3)

Puzzle #36

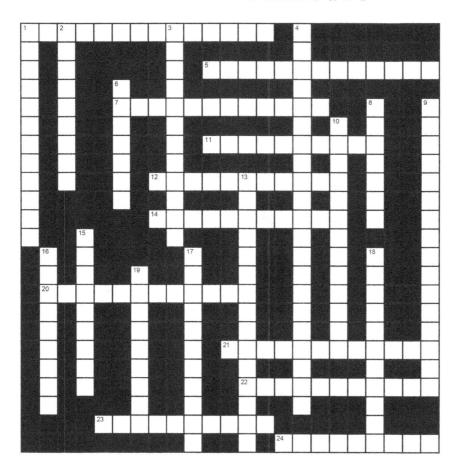

Across

1 Round Mound of Rebound (7,7)
5 Beat HOU in the 1981 NBA Finals (6,7)
7 First black player to get signed by team but never played (6,6)
11 Highest winning percentage as a coach in Hornets history, 1996-1999 (4,6)
12 2022 Defensive player of year (6,5)
14 HBO miniseries on rise of the Lakers in the 1980s (7,4)
20 City of Golden State Warriors (3,9)
21 A player reaches double digits in 2 offensive categories in a game (6,6)
22 Team that had 10-game winning and losing streaks in same season (7,4)
23 2017 AND 2018 DPOY UTA (4,6)
24 First black player to play in NBA (4,5)

Down

1 Won the 1996 Finals vs SEA (7,5)
2 Michael Jordan nickname (3,6)
3 1st Pelican to score 2,000 points in a season (7,5)
4 Team founded in 1989 (9,12)
6 Oscar Robertson nickname (3,3,1)
8 76ers conference (7)
9 Beat the Pacers in the 2000 NBA Finals (3,7,6)
10 1969 MVP Baltimore (7,6)
13 Won the 1999 NBA Finals vs the Knicks (3,7,5)
15 longest losing streak in a single season (6,3)
16 Holds Mavs single season assist record (5,4)
17 Bulls coach 1989-1998 (4,7)
18 Celtics player who had 50 rebounds in a game (4,7)
19 Scored 60 points against the Hawks in 1985, BOS (5,4)

Puzzle #37

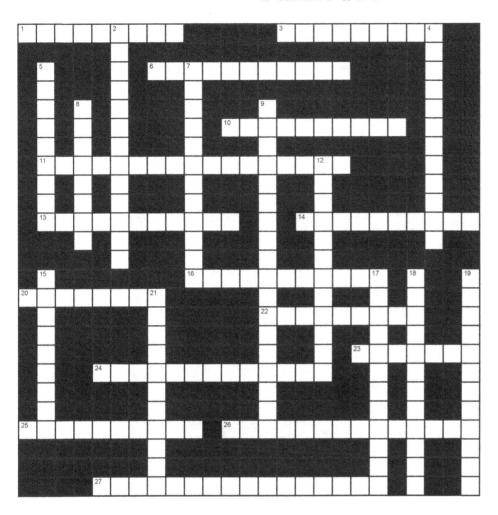

Across

1. HOF player, Pacers coach with highest career win % (5,4)
3. Timberwolves division (9)
6. Averaged a triple double in the 2017 Finals (6,5)
10. 1st Celtic to make 1,000 career 3 pointers (4,6)
11. Most blocked shots in Bucks history (6,5-6)
13. 2009 ROY CHI (7,4)
14. Giannis nickname (5,5)
16. 2022 MVP (6,5)
20. 1982 ROY, Nets, Buck (8)
22. 1st Pistons player with 10 triple doubles in season (5,4)
23. Raptors conference (7)
24. 1988 MVP CHI (7,6)
25. 1st player to make 400 3 pointers in a season (5,5)
26. Brook Lopez's nickname (6,8)
27. Beat the Pistons in the 1988 NBA Finals (3,7,6)

Down

2. Beat the Suns in the 1976 NBA Finals (6,7)
4. Made playoffs every year from 1997-2004, never made Finals (12)
5. Led the league in triple doubles his rookie season, Mavs (5,4)
7. Florida coach in 06 and 07 championship seasons (5,7)
8. Chris Webber traded from Magic to (8)
9. Dominique Wilkins nickname (5,9,4)
12. Mavs coach with highest win%, fired after 2008 season (5,7)
15. Team Mavs lost to in 2006 Finals and then beat in 2011 Finals (5,4)
17. Won their 3rd straight title in 1993 (7,5)
18. Wilt Chamberlain nickname (4,3,5)
19. 2004 MVP MIN (5,7)
21. Country Steve Nash was born in (5,6)

Puzzle #38

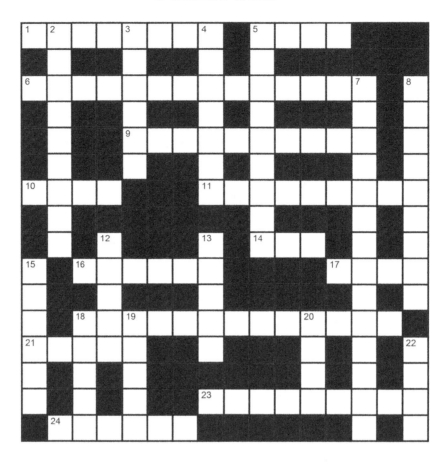

Across

1 Pistons, Bill (8)
5 LeBron led the Cavs to ____ straight Finals after returning (4)
6 Won their 2nd straight title in 1990 vs Portland (7,7)
9 2000 Co-ROY CHI (5,5)
10 A deceptive move by the offense (4)
11 Warriors coach (5,4)
14 Free throw and foul line area (3)
16 Moving more than two steps without dribbling (6)
17 Heat big 3, LeBron, Wade, and _____ (4)
18 Pass made behind the body (6,3,4)
21 MIA, Tyler (5)
23 Movie Kevin Garnett appeared in alongside Adam Sandler (5,4)
24 1969 ROY, Bullets, Westley (6)

Down

2 Nets original team name (9)
3 Suns, Devin (6)
4 Toronto (7)
5 An offensive sprint down the court after a rebound or steal (4,5)
7 Won first two DPOY awards, Bucks (6,8)
8 NOVA coach, recently retired (3,6)
12 NBA 75 Team, PHI, Hal (5)
13 Walt "____" Frazier (5)
15 Lakers PG Derek (6)
18 Downtown Freddie _____ (5)
19 Pistons mascot animal (5)
20 bad high draft pick (4)
22 Lakers family ownership (4)

Puzzle #39

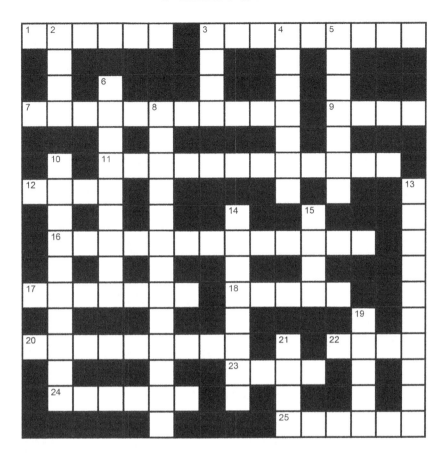

Across

1. Pistons retired number 4, Joe (6)
3. A basket made (5,4)
7. 2018 MVP HOU (5,6)
9. 1979 ROY, Kings, Phil (4)
11. 1981 MVP PHI (6,6)
12. Lakers championships during the 1980s (4)
16. BC (6,7)
17. Knicks (3,4)
18. Shot that goes straight through net without touching rim or backboard (5)
20. 53 double-doubles in a row during 2010-2011 season, MIN (5,4)
22. Mike Breen 3 point call (4)
23. 1965 ROY, NYK, Willis (4)
24. MEM, Ja (6)
25. Kareem broke his hand punching this teammate, Kent (6)

Down

2. Kareem played college basktball here (4)
3. Steve Kerr has coached the Warriors to _____ championships (4)
4. SAS, TOR, LAC Kawhi (7)
5. Clippers, Nets Blake (7)
6. Nets played here before Brooklyn (3,6)
8. Center line dividing the court (4,5,4)
10. HOF Syracuse coach (3,7)
13. Wizards (10)
14. Gene Hackman basketball movie (8)
15. Brooklyn (4)
19. 1st Mavs player to have number retired, #15 Brad (5)
21. Spud (4)

Puzzle #40

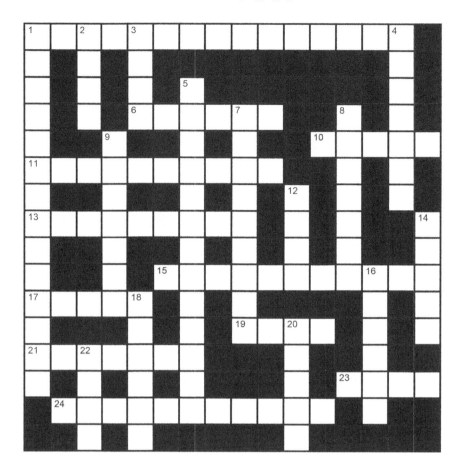

Across

1. Bucks coach (4,11)
6. Giannis country (6)
10. 8 steals in a quarter, Fat (5)
11. Lakers (3,7)
13. 1959 MVP St. Louis (3,6)
15. HOF Pistons PG (5,6)
17. To play defense on an opposing player (5)
19. PHO (4)
21. Team in possession of ball (7)
23. Another word for basket (4)
24. Thunder originally the _____ (11)

Down

1. 2017 ROY Bucks (7,7)
2. Longtime Nuggets coach, George (4)
3. NBA 75 Team, DET, Dave (4)
4. Houston (7)
5. Philadelphia (7-6)
7. Chest to chest pass with both hands (5,4)
8. Will Ferrell basketball movie (4,3)
9. Blocked 8 shots in a quarter GS, Erick (7)
12. Miami (4)
14. 6th man of the year, 1995 NYK, Anthony (5)
16. Led the league in scoring 3 straight seasons, Clippers, Bob (6)
18. Nuggets (6)
20. Suns single season block record, Larry (5)
22. An illegal play (4)

Puzzle #41

Across

5 "Big Nasty" Pistons, 2002 6th man of the year (7,10)
9 NYK Charles (6)
10 Malice at the _____ (6)
11 Moses (6)
12 Blocked 8 shots in a quarter PHI (7,7)
15 Brad Stevens coached at this college (6)
16 MIN high draft pick PG, Ricky (5)
17 Sixers single season assist record, 1986, Maurice (6)
19 HOF Duke, Grant (4)
20 Also known as weak side (4,4)
22 2nd pick in 2000 draft, Stromile (5)
23 OKC record 10 threes in a game (4,6)
24 SAS (5)
25 Latrell (8)

Down

1 HOF Celtics, Kevin (2,5)
2 TOR, Pascal (6)
3 2003 ROY Suns (5,10)
4 CBB (7,10)
6 POR, Damian (7)
7 Kareem signature shot (7)
8 Won the 2010 NBA Finals vs BOS (3,7,6)
13 PG Donovan (8)
14 Lakers HOF, James (6)
18 Red Auerbach was known for smoking these after victories (6)
21 Dunk alternative (5)

Puzzle #42

Across

1. Timberwolves mascot (6,3,4)
6. Coach, Byron (5)
9. Bulls arena (6,6)
10. MIA, Bam (7)
12. Grizzlies (7)
15. Spurs coach (5,8)
17. Clippers (3,7)
18. Most blocks by player in single game (17), LAL Elmore (5)
19. Movie staring Ray Allen, directed by Spike Lee (2,3,4)
21. Side of the court where the live ball is absent (4,4)
22. LAL, NOP, Brandon (6)

Down

2. Shot free throws underhand, GS (4,5)
3. BKN (4)
4. Shot clock length in the NBA (6,4,7)
5. First round picks Clippers traded for Paul George (4)
7. NBA commisioner (4,6)
8. Big Ticket (5,7)
11. The NBA originally had ____ teams (5)
13. HOF Celtics, Kevin (6)
14. Alonzo (8)
16. Mavericks got their name from a (2,4)
17. Won 2020 Finals in the bubble vs MIA (6)
20. Yao (4)

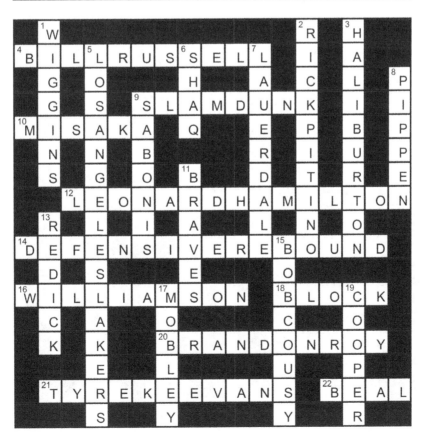

3

Crossword puzzle with the following filled entries:

Across:
- 3: HOLMGREN
- 5: STOUDAMIRE
- 7: EIGHT
- 9: BEARD
- 11: SANANTONIO
- 13/14: INTENTIONALFOUL
- 15: STEVENASH
- 21: KOBEBRYANT
- 22: SLAMDUNK
- 23: DENVERNUGGETS
- 24: SUNS

Down:
- 1: D
- 2: M
- 3: HAMMELT
- 6: OFFENSE
- 8: GR
- 10: P, A, R, B, F
- 12: MILES
- 13: JASON
- 14: INVERTED (?)
- 15: STEVE (down from 15)
- 16: NERD (N, E, D, F)
- 17: GEE
- 18: DR
- 19: PAL
- 20: LAKERS
- 21: KID

4

Crossword puzzle with the following filled entries:

Across:
- 1: SHOTCLOCK
- 6: SUNS
- 7: ROBERTSON
- 9: DELL
- 10: MARQUETTE
- 11: BUCKS
- 13: JABSTEP
- 15: LEPRECHAUN
- 17: COURT
- 19: PALMING
- 20: BROWN
- 21: BOBHUGGINS
- 22: THIRTYTHREE

Down:
- 1: SPUEWE
- 2: LO
- 3: KAREEM
- 4: PE
- 5: HUSSE
- 6: SLICE
- 8: ARI
- 10: MAADE
- 12: UBRY
- 14: J
- 16: ENGLLS
- 18: KNIGHTS

5

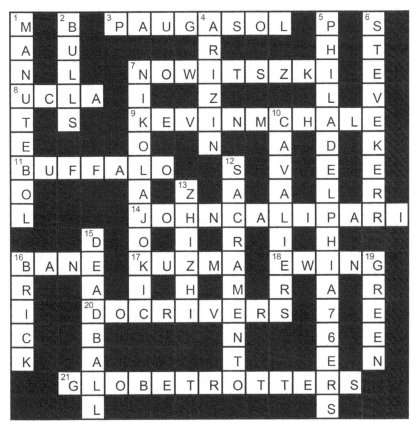

6

7

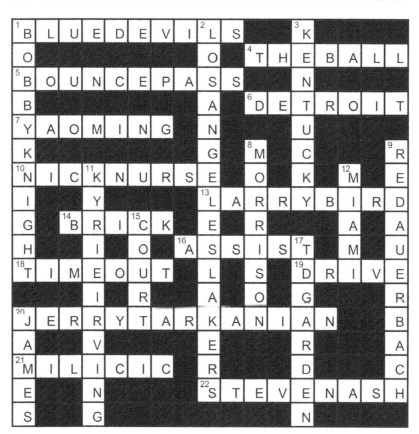

8

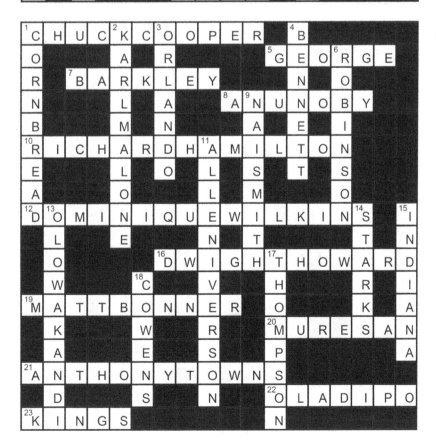

11

	1	2						3				4
	S	U	B	S	T	I	T	U	T	E		J	A	Z	Z			C
			A					O				U
		5 N	E	6 W	Y	O	R	7 K	K	N	I	C	K	8 S		R
			A		E			A				E		I		R
9 C	H	A	N	D	L	E	R		W			10 M	A	X	E	Y
L			T		L				H				T
I		11 P	O	S	S	E	S	S	I	O	12 N		13 H		13 L
P			N		F				L		A		14 M		A
15 P	E	L	I	C	A	N	S		E		T		O		A		R
E			O		R		16 R	O	B	I	N	S	O	N		R
R			S		G				N		O		E			Y
17 S	A	M	P	S	O	N		18 B	A	R	N	E	S			O
			U		C		19 B		R		A		M			B
		20 K	A	R	E	E	M	A	B	D	U	L	J	A	B	B	A	R
			S		N		Y				S		L			I
			T				L						O			E
		21 C	A	R	M	E	L	O	A	N	T	H	O	N	Y		N
					R		R						E

12

	1	2		3		4		5
K	A	N	S	A	S	C	I	T	Y		K	O	R	V	E	R
				L		Y					I
	6 J	O	H	N	H	A	V	L	I	C	E	K		7 K		R
				R		E					A		G
							8 K	Y	R	I	E	I	R	V	I	N	G
9 D	R	10 A	K	E			S		H				L		N
W		S				11 R	O	B	E	R	12 T	P	A	R	I	S	H		13 H
I		S		14 C		N			R		I		N		A
G		I		L		15 J	R	S	M	I	T	H		H		Y
H		S		Y		O			B		H				E
T		T		D		16 S			E		O				S
H					17 K	E	V	I	N	D	U	R	A	N	T
O		18 M				D			W		Y		19 B		20 G
W		U			21 F	R	O	N	T	C	O	U	R	T
22 A	I	R	B	A	L	L			L		O		X		I
R		R			I				V		W		O		N
23 D	R	A	Y	M	O	N	D	G	R	E	E	N		U		E
		Y			E				S		S			T		R

13

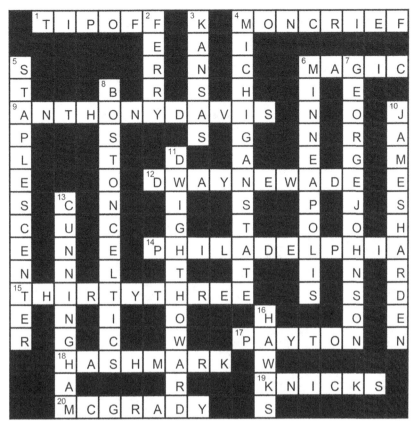

14

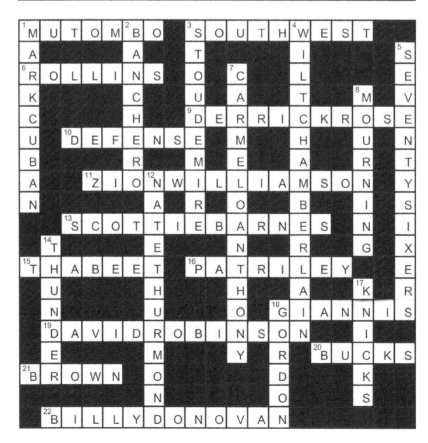

17

Across:
1. BROWN
3. LOWPOST
7. CARRYING
9. BLAKEGRIFFIN
11. BILLWALTON
13. BENNETT
14. PJWASHINGTON
16. SIMMONS
19. KEVINDURANT
20. MOSESMALONE
21. MONROE
22. BULLS
23. EASTERN
24. PACERS

18

Across:
1. LAKERS
2. CHRISPAUL
6. BUCKS
7. WILKES
9. SHAQUILLEONEAL
11. JAMALCRAWFORD
14. AIRBALL
16. THIRTYFOUR
20. DEROZAN
21. REBOUND
22. ALLENIVERSON

19

20

21

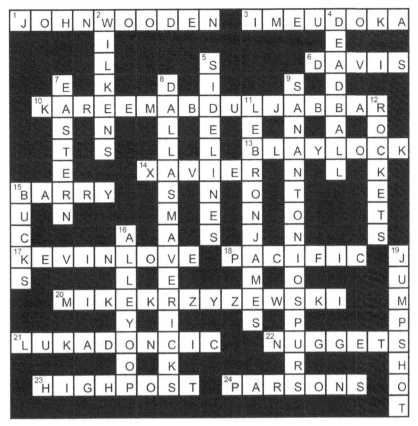

22

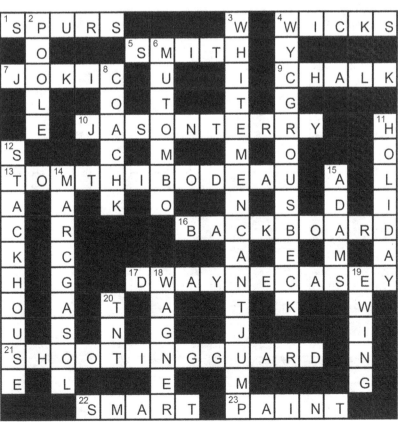

23

24

25

Across:
- 1. LARRY JOHNSON
- 4. NUGGETS
- 7. CHAPMAN
- 9. ROY WILLIAMS
- 11. MIAMI HEAT
- 13. NORTHWEST
- 15. EASTERN
- 20. FLIP SAUNDERS
- 21. WILKINS
- 22. DIRK NOWITZKI
- 23. MICHAEL JORDAN
- 24. DAVID THOMPSON

26

Across:
- 1. HELD BALL
- 3. TIM DUNCAN
- 6. RAY ALLEN
- 7. BANK SHOT
- 11. MAGIC JOHNSON
- 13. HOLDING
- 14. WILLIAMS
- 15. CHAUNCEY BILLUPS
- 18. THREE POINTER
- 20. CELTICS
- 21. HORNETS
- 22. SHAWN BRADLEY
- 23. WARRIORS
- 24. DAN GILBERT

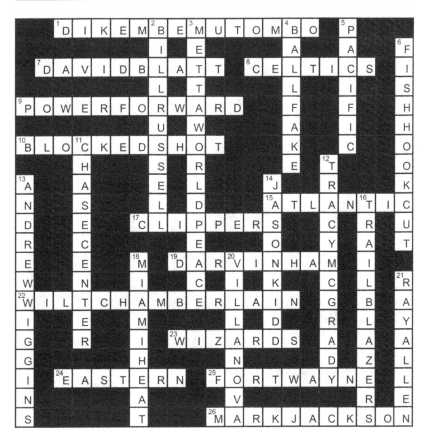

31

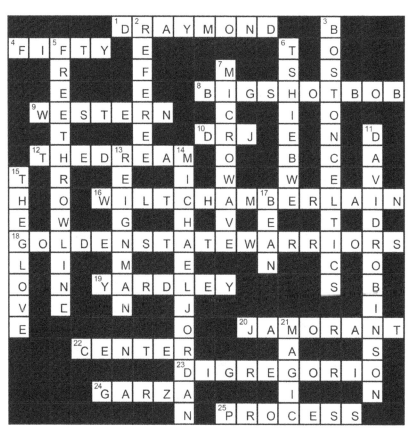

32

33

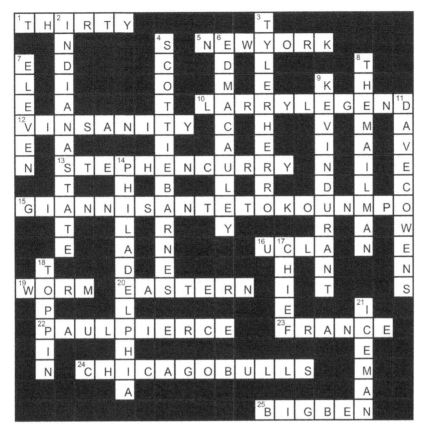

34

35

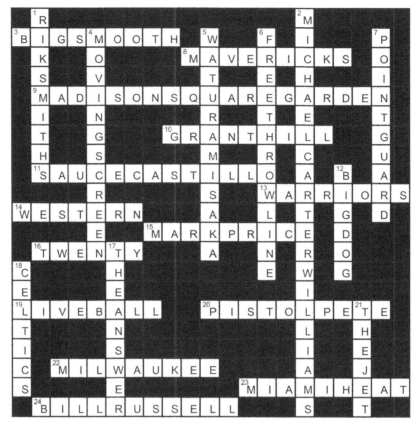

36

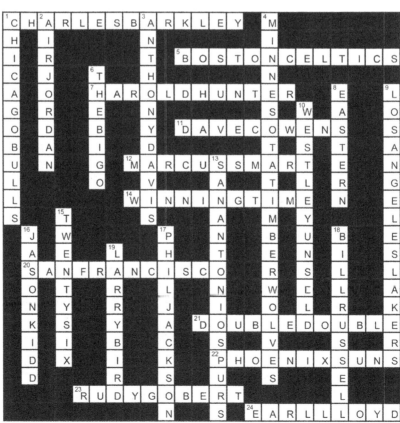

37

38

39

40

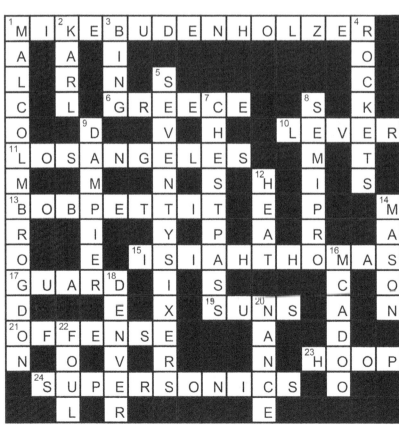

41

Across:
- 5. CORLISSWILLIAMSON
- 9. OAKLEY
- 10. PALACE
- 11. MALONE
- 12. DIKEMBEMUTOMBO
- 15. BUTLER
- 16. RUBIO
- 17. CHEEKS
- 19. HILL
- 20. HELPSIDE
- 22. SWIFT
- 23. PAULGEORGE
- 24. SPURS
- 25. SPREWELL

Down:
- 1. KJONES
- 2. S
- 3. A
- 4. COLLEGE
- 6. LIKELY
- 7. SKHO
- 8. WOASKARL
- 10. PNG
- 13. MILK
- 14. WORT
- 15. BCS
- 17. CMEBAL
- 18. C
- 21. LAYUR

42

Across:
- 1. CRUNCHTHEWOLF
- 6. SCOTT
- 9. UNITEDCENTER
- 10. ADEBAYO
- 12. MEMPHIS
- 15. GREGGPOPOVICH
- 17. LOSANGELES
- 18. SMITH
- 19. HEGOTGAME
- 21. WEAKSIDE
- 22. INGRAM

Down:
- 1. CSKBSY
- 2. RIES
- 3. NEST
- 4. TWE
- 5. FIV
- 7. AADAAL
- 8. KRVNGARNETT
- 11. BIHT
- 13. CCHALL
- 14. MSC
- 16. TVSHO
- 17. LAKCRN
- 20. MEIN

Made in the USA
Monee, IL
14 December 2023

49304505R00037